M000079732

How
to Be
Happy,
Though
Married

Published in 2007 by
Chicago Review Press, Incorporated
814 North Franklin Street
Chicago, Illinois 60610

ISBN-13: 978-1-55652-699-2
ISBN-10: 1-55652-699-7

How to Be Happy, Though Married
A Tender Compendium of Good *and Bad* Advice

Compiled by Michelle Lovric
Designed by Michelle Lovric and Lisa Pentreath
Concept and compilation copyright © 2007
Michelle Lovric
www.michellelovric.com
Editorial Assistant: Kristina Blagojevitch
Printed in China by Imago

10 9 8 7 6 5 4 3 2 1

How
to Be
Happy,
Though
Married

**A Tender Compendium of
Good *and Bad* Advice**

Compiled by Michelle Lovric

CHICAGO
REVIEW
PRESS

Preliminaries

Love and sex are nature's salesmen.

Anne B. Fisher

Most women I know wouldn't know a good man if he came up, bit them on the nose and left his address to forward the police report to.

Mariella Frostrup

Marriage is not something that can be accomplished all at once; it has to be constantly reaccomplished.

André Maurois

I believe a little incompatibility is the spice of life, particularly if he has income and she is pattable.

Ogden Nash

A wife is like a blanket: cover yourself, it irritates you; cast it aside, you feel cold.

Ghanaian proverb

The bonds of matrimony are like any other bonds – they mature slowly.

Peter De Vries

When I get invited to a wedding I always give the newlyweds a £50 voucher for a firm of solicitors that I know.

Jenny Eclair

Contents

Whatever Is Delightful *in* Human Life

I am verily persuaded that whatever is delightful in human life, is to be enjoyed in greater perfection in the married than in the single condition.

The Matrimonial Preceptor, 1765

The word "marriage" serves only to mask the most flattering of ideas.

Giacomo Girolamo Casanova, *History of My Life*, completed in 1798

Everybody is liable to get married; it is a phenomenon, like measles or the common cold.

Margaret Cole, *Marriage Past and Present*, 1938

It's *true* "the pickings are lean" but it only takes one, just one measly man out of all those millions and millions.

Helen Gurley Brown

Never conceive of yourself as complete without the other half of yourself.

Edward Turner, *The Young Man's Companion, or, Friendly Adviser,* 1861

It isn't just finding the right person; it's being the right person.

Anthony Cotterell, *The Expert Way of Getting Married*, 1939

Whatever Is Delightful *in* Human Life

It is true that there have been memorable celibates, but in the main the world's work has been done by the married.

Reverend E. J. Hardy, *How to Be Happy Though Married*, 1886

Modern romantic love marriage is, in fact, the most daring experiment yet tried by human beings.

Mary Borden, *The Technique of Marriage*, 1933

Marriage is not only a very natural, but a very beautiful, way of increasing love.

Annie H. Ryder, *Hold Up Your Heads, Girls! Helps for Girls, in School and Out,* 1886

Most of us become aware sooner or later that to have one true, warm-hearted, completely devoted comrade is worth all the wealth and all the fame which the world can offer.

David R. Mace

To be well married is heaven; to be ill married is the other place which it is not polite to mention.

James Riding, *Heads and Hearts, Being Advice on Courtship and Marriage*, 1893

Different marriages work in different ways. Adolf Hitler and Eva Braun got married, spent one day in a bomb shelter and then committed suicide together. Fine; if that's what they found worked best for them.

John O'Farrell

How to *Choose* a Mate

Marriage is a sack full of ninety-nine snakes and one eel.

Spanish proverb

Simple instinct can no more be trusted as the guide of love than we could trust it in the building of a ship, or in playing a symphony of Beethoven.

Anna Longshore-Potts, *Lecture on Courtship: or, Hearts and Homes*, 1861

Horses, asses, cattle, even slaves of the smallest worth, clothes, kettles, wooden seats, cups, and earthenware pitchers, are first tried and then bought: a wife is the only thing that is not shown before she is married, for fear she may not give satisfaction.

Saint Jerome, *Against Jovinian*, 393

I never have been able to make up my mind whether ideal love was the best, or if love with a great deal of common sense in it was not the most philosophical and better in the long run. But to those of us who are romantic it is fearful to think of deliberately turning our backs on terrapin and lobster and ice cream, and meditating upon plain bread and cold potatoes.

Lilian Bell, *From a Girl's Point of View*, 1897

I beg you not to "settle."

Helen Gurley Brown

Husband-hunting girls are a foolish race of sportswomen and apt to waste powder and shot indiscriminately.

Augusta Webster, *A Housewife's Opinions*, 1879

How to *Choose* a Mate

The matrimonial enterprises of the more reflective and analytical sort of women are almost always directed to men whose lack of pulchritude makes them easier to bring down, and, what is more important still, easier to hold down.

H. L. Mencken, *In Defense of Women*, 1918

I can tell you where you might look for your mojo, darling, but the miracle man? If I knew that, I'd have my own magazine called *Spare Blokes*, which I'd run from the poolside of the Cipriani while a few of the hand-picked Italian brotherhood polished my sunglasses.

Marion McBride

A woman never pursues a man – but then a mousetrap doesn't pursue a mouse either.

Ronnie Barker

I've gone for each type: the rough guy; the nerdy, sweet, lovable guy; and the slick guy. I don't really have a type. Men in general are a good thing.

Jennifer Aniston

Going by my track record, if I'd met a Mr Darcy, he wouldn't have found me brilliant or feisty; he'd have taken steps to have me sectioned.

Barbara Ellen

How to *Choose* a Mate

Young persons are often hasty in contracting marriage; too much disposed to accept the first offer, whether it be good or bad, lest they should be compelled to lead a life of single blessedness.

Nelson Sizer, *Thoughts on Domestic Life: or, Marriage Vindicated*, 1858

It is a fact that giving advice to a woman in love is about as effective as talking sense to a hell-bent lemming.

Irma Kurtz

The truth is that there are thousands of people with whom each of us could enjoy a decent relationship, sprinkled across the globe like glitter.

Mariella Frostrup

It's *probably* better to be single in your twenties and thirties when a lot of people have the hots for you and you can have as many affairs as you care to, and married when you're old and not so *many* people want you.

Helen Gurley Brown

Disparity in descent, fortunes, friends, do often beget a distraction in the mind. Disparity of years breeds dislike, obscurity of descent begets contempt, and inequality of fortunes discontent.

Hannah Woolley, *The Gentlewoman's Companion or, a Guide to the Female Sex*, 1675

How to *Choose* a Mate

Beauty and the Beast may be a pretty fairy-tale, but in the realism of practical life it assumes the guise of a tragedy that makes the looker-on shudder with disgustful pity.

Marion Harland, *The Secret of a Happy Home*, 1896

It is hardwired in the male psyche to trade up whenever possible – the "Am I out of my league?" chip mysteriously going astray when opportunity beckons.

Barbara Ellen

What we [men] want for the most part is a humble, flattering, smiling, child-loving, tea-making being, who laughs at our jokes however old they may be, coaxes and wheedles us in our humours, and fondly lies to us through life.

William Makepeace Thackeray, *The Book of Snobs, and, Sketches and Travels in London*, 1869

Go down the ladder when thou marriest a wife; go up when thou choosest a friend.

Rabbi Shimon Ben Azai, 1st century

Believe in no "affinity" which you do not comprehend. Surrender to no blind impulse, and loiter not in the sphere of mysterious attraction.

George Stearns, *Love and Mock Love*, 1860

By candlelight, a goat looks like a lady.

French proverb

How to *Choose* a Mate

. . . *Beauty vs* Brains

To love at first look makes a house of misrule.

Hannah Woolley

If her beauty intoxicates you, take a glance at her grandmother.

Godfrey Poage, *What You Ought to Know Before Marriage*, 1950

While it is frequently natural and right to love a "beautiful" woman, to love a woman because she is beautiful is as unreasonable as to fall in love with a beautiful statue.

Havelock Ellis, *Impressions and Comments*, 1914–24

Beauty . . . is likely to produce vanity, and vanity, besides several other disagreeable features, leads to extravagance. I won't stop to tell you what extravagance leads to.

Casper S. Yost, *The Making of a Successful Husband, Letters of a Happily Married Man to His Son*, 1908

If she looks old, she's old. If she looks young, she's young. If she looks back, follow her.

Bob Hope

When a young lady has angelic features, eats nothing to speak of, plays all day long on the piano, and sings ravishingly in church . . . she may be a little devil after all. Yet so it is: she may be a tale-bearer, a liar, and a thief; she may have a taste for brandy, and no heart.

Robert Louis Stevenson, *Virginibus Puerisque*, 1881

How to *Choose* a Mate

. . . Beauty vs Brains

There are women, who, on the surface, look like really hot stuff.
. . . But underneath the lip gloss and the Wonderbra lies the libido
of a Giant Panda. These are the girls who collect cuddly toys.

Jenny Eclair

"Some men marry dimples, some ears; some noses; the
contest, however, generally lies between the eyes and the hair.
The mouth, too, is occasionally married; the chin not so often.
. . . Young ladies do also make some queer matches, and unite
themselves to whiskers."

J. W. Kirton quoting a contemporary newspaper article,
*Happy Homes, and How to Make Them; or, Counsels on Love,
Courtship, and Marriage*, 1870

I've always been drawn to shallow.

Hugh Grant

The great use of female beauty, the great practical advantage
of it is, that it naturally and unavoidably tends to *keep the
husband in good humour with himself*, to make him, to use the
dealer's phrase, *pleased with his bargain*.

William Cobbett, *Advice to Young Men*, 1829

An ugly Wife is a common Trouble, but may be eased many
times in a day; that is, as often as the Husband goes out of her
sight.

Don Francisco Manuel de Mello, *The Government of a Wife; or,
Wholsom and Pleasant Advice for Married Men*, 1637

How to *Choose* a Mate

. . . Beauty vs Brains

Phrenological Choices

Means of ascertaining how much Affection a Person has:
This is indicated by the development of the head behind the ears. If, therefore, a young lady wants an affectionate husband, let her, before she accepts his hand, make an examination of the back of his head. Get him to stand so that you get a view of his head in profile, and then see how full the head is generally behind; and if it is anything like fig 2 [a man with a flat head] you had better have nothing to do with him. . . .

Supposing, for instance, figures 5 and 6 were to marry, they would not be at all well matched. She has a high head, which indicates a lofty moral nature; while his head is low, especially in front, indicating that his moral nature is very weak. She is large in Conscientiousness, is disposed to be honest, truthful, upright, and straightforward; but he is small in Conscientiousness, and would be dishonest and unscrupulous – he would cheat and swindle whenever he got the chance. She would be disgusted at his want of principle, while he would regard her as foolishly particular. . . . In years to come, when the exceeding usefulness of Phrenology, as applied to the selection of husbands and wives, is fully realized, it will, I feel sure, be quite the usual thing for intending partners to consult a phrenologist before entering into an engagement. When this time arrives, happy marriages, instead of being the exception, as it is to be feared is at present the case, will become the rule.

Professor Durham, *Husbands and Wives, How to Select Them Phrenologically and Live Happily When Married*, 1889

The average stature of the man is about three inches greater than that of the woman, and in the physiologic marriage any great deviation from this should be avoided.

Anna M. Galbraith, *The Four Epochs of Woman's Life*, 1901

How to *Choose* a Mate
. . . Beauty vs Brains

Significance of Moles in a Future Partner

A Mole on the Belly denotes Whoredom, Luxury and Gluttony.

A Mole on the Lip signifies the Party to be much beloved and very amorous.

A Mole on the left Buttock denotes a pleasing person very much delighted in the work of Generation.

A Mole on the Ankle, in a Man, denotes Effeminacy; but in a Woman, a masculine Spirit, and that She shall wear the Breeches.

A Mole on the right Thigh foretells Riches and Advancement by Marriage; and on the private Parts it doth the like.

The Amorous Gallant's Tongue Tipp'd with Golden Expressions or,
The Art of Courtship Refined, 1741

The following patterns left in a tea-cup bode well or ill for marriage:

Pears.—Improved social condition and other advantages; this fruit brings success to a business man and to a woman a rich husband.

Castle.—You may expect fortune to smile upon you; a crumbling castle denotes disappointment and ill success in love and marriage.

Easel.—A sign of marriage to widows and maids.

Man Carrying a Burden.—An unhappy marriage or an unfortunate love affair.

Peacock.—A sign of the acquisition of property; a prosperous and happy marriage.

Whip.—To a woman this sign foretells vexation and trials in her marriage.

Quill Pen, Lilies of the Valley, An Organ.—Great happiness through marriage.

Violet, A Water Lily, A Robin, A Crescent Moon, A Ring.—A romantic love affair which ends in a happy marriage taking place in the early spring.

Cicely Kent, *Telling Fortunes by Tea Leaves,* 1922

How to *Choose* a Mate
. . . What to Look for in *Her*

If you want to know how your girl will treat you after marriage, just listen to her talking to her little brother.

Sam Levenson

If a girl is too easily kissable, the man is apt to think she is just as familiar with others and that thought takes a great discount off her value.

"Madame Elise," *Secrets of Fascination*, 1906

Women, that like the River *Nile*, have their Origin unknown, and it cannot be found whence they come, are as much to be avoided as the Crocodils [sic] that River breeds.

Don Francisco Manuel de Mello

But the girl who comes from a bad family; whose body is either very short or very tall, very fat or very thin; whose skin is ever rough and hard; whose hair and eyes are yellowish, the latter like a cat's; whose teeth are long, or are wholly wanting; whose mouth and lips are wide and projecting, with the lower lip of a dark colour, and tremulous when speaking, who allows her tongue to loll out; whose eyebrows are straight; whose temples are depressed; who shows signs of beard, mustachios, and dense body-pile; whose neck is thick . . . whose one breast is large or high, and the other low or small, whose ears are triangular, like a sifting or winnowing fan; whose second toe is larger and longer than the big toe; whose third toe is blunt . . . should be carefully avoided, under all circumstances, by the wise.

Kalyana Malla, *The Ananga Ranga, or The Hindu Art of Love*, 16th century

How to *Choose* a Mate
. . . What to Look for in *Her*

One that hath a thick and smooth face is slothful and given to pleasures. . . . A little straight forehead denotes an unbridled appetite in lust. . . . Little ears demonstrate aptness to venery. . . . A woman that hath a long nose is lustful . . . if women have beards, being not very old, their lust is not to be satisfied. Little breasts in women are a greater sign of lust, than great ones. But if men have them great, it signifies the contrary. They that have much hair about the privy members are lustful, because it denotes that they abound with much fumy heat . . .

Giovanni Sinibaldi, *Rare Verities, the Cabinet of Venus Unlock'd*, 1658

The signs of chastity are as follows: shame, modesty, fear, a faultless gait and speech, casting eyes down before men and the acts of men. Some women are so clever, however, that they know how to resist detection by these signs, and in this case a man should turn to their urine. The urine of virgins is clear and lucid, sometimes white, sometimes sparkling.

Pseudo-Albertus Magnus, *De Secretis Mulierum*, c. 1478

The woman who bears on the sole of her left foot a line extending from the "mount" or cushion of the little toe, to the ball of the big toe, that woman will readily obtain a good husband. . . . The maiden whose neck is very long, will be of a wicked and cruel disposition. The maiden whose neck is very short, will be wretchedly poor. . . . The maiden whose palms have lines in the shape of an Ankush (spiked hook for guiding elephants), a Kuntala (a spur), and a Chakra (quoit or discus), will intermarry with a royal house and bear a son who shows the most fortunate signs.

Kalyana Malla

How to *Choose* a Mate
. . . What to Look for in *Her*

But, *who is to tell* whether a girl will make an industrious woman? . . . It was a story in Philadelphia, some years ago, that a young man, who was courting one of three sisters, happened to be on a visit to her, when all the three were present, and when one said to the others, "I *wonder* where *our* needle is." Upon which he withdrew, as soon as was consistent with the rules of politeness, resolved never to think more of a girl who possessed a needle only in partnership, and who, it appeared, was not too well informed as to the place where even that share was deposited.

William Cobbett

When choosing a wife a man should, without letting her know that she was being tested, ask the girl he is thinking of to find something belonging to her in the dark. If she is, as she ought to be, a centre of order, she will easily be able to do so.

Reverend E. J. Hardy, *The Five Talents of Women*, 1888

If a girl desires to woo you, before allowing her to press her suit, ask her if she knows how to press yours.

Stephen Leacock, *Literary Lapses*, 1910

Certainly, if I could help it, I would never marry a wife who wrote. The practice of letters is miserably harassing to the mind; and after an hour or two's work, all the more human portion of the author is extinct.

Robert Louis Stevenson

18

How to *Choose* a Mate

. . . What to Look for in *Her*

A young man of very good brains was telling me, the other day, his dreams of his future wife. Rattling on, more in joke than in earnest, he said, "She must be perfectly ignorant, and a bigot: she must know nothing, and believe everything. I should wish to have her from the adjoining room call to me, 'My dear, what do two and two make?'" . . . As for two and two, I should say that it had always been the habit of women to ask that question of some man, and to rest easily satisfied with the answer. They have generally called, as my friend wished, from some other room, saying, "My dear, what do two and two make?" and the husband or father or brother has answered and said, "My dear, they make four for a man, and three for a woman."

Thomas Wentworth Higginson, *Women and the Alphabet*, 1881

19

Watch out for the dieter. She may be lovely and streamlined to feast your eyes on, but facing the future with a girl who is mad on keeping thin has wrecked many a man.

Anne B. Fisher, *All Done by Kindness, Hints on Deportment for the Marriage Ring*, 1938

The mere whisper that a girl collects prints, stamps, tropical fish or African art is, alas, likely to increase her solitude.

Frank Crowninshield

Desperation is a bad look, no matter how you accessorize it.

Mariella Frostrup

How to *Choose* a Mate
. . . What to Look for in *Him*

Marry a nice man. Since life is out there handing you so many horrors, how can you cope if the biggest horror of them all is him?

Helen Gurley Brown

A husband should not be an impulsive or accidental acquisition. No woman buys the first gown she sees when she steps into a shop. . . . A girl should choose, first of all, a MAN in every sense of the word. Not a mere appendage to a cigarette; not a lounge lizard; not a perambulating stockticker; not an animated booze receptacle; not a whited sepulchre of disease and corruption.

Bernarr Adolphus MacFadden, *Be Married and Like It*, 1937

Never think for one moment of the society of any other than a good man. Whatever may be his extrinsic endowments – wit, beauty, talent, rank, property or prospects – all should be as nothing to you, unless his character is what it should be. . . . A close examination, as with the microscope, will disclose irregularity and roughness on the most polished or smooth surface.

William A. Alcott, *A Young Woman's Guide*, 1845

The man whose eye is red, whose body is fair and has a good complexion like gold; whose trunk is fleshy and whose arms reach his knees, the same will always remain rich and enjoy grandeur, opulence, lordship and supremacy.

The man whose thighs are large, will win great wealth; the man whose waist is broad, will be blessed in his wife and many children. . . . The man whose Linga is very long, will be wretchedly poor. The man whose Linga is very thick, will ever be in distress . . . and the man whose Linga is short, will be a Rajah.

Kalyana Malla

How to *Choose* a Mate
. . . What to Look for in *Him*

Men of a low or short composure of body, enjoy a more quick and piercing sense of venereal pleasure, than tall men.

Giovanni Sinibaldi

Men who fish, botanize, work with the turning-lathe, or gather seaweeds, will make admirable husbands and a little amateur painting in watercolour shows the innocent and quiet mind. Those who have a few intimates are to be avoided; while those who swim loose, who have their hat in their hand all along the street, who can number an infinity of acquaintances and are not chargeable with any one friend, promise an easy disposition and no rival to the wife's influence. . . . Lastly (and this is, perhaps, the golden rule), no woman should marry a teetotaller.

Robert Louis Stevenson

There are men, and not a few of them, who are doomed to disappointment in marriage. . . . They married with the idea that in such a union the grossest lust would have the sanction of the law. These men who stare decency out of countenance upon the street, who lay traps for the ruin of innocent and unsuspecting girls, who invade the sanctity of the home, and whose course through life is like the slimy trail of a venomous serpent, are unfit for marriage – they are unfit to be regarded even as men.

Sylvanus Stall, *What a Young Husband Ought to Know*, 1900

Avoid a companion that may entail any hereditary disease on your posterity, particularly that most dreadful of all human calamities, madness.

The Female Instructor; or, Young Woman's Companion, 1811

How to *Choose* a Mate

Many girls lust after what they can't get and hate what's offered on a plate.

Ovid, *Ars Amatoria*, 1st century BC

The problem with people who have no vices is that generally you can be pretty sure they're going to have some pretty annoying virtues.

Elizabeth Taylor

Decide what you want him for – sex? Companionship? Protection? Show? And don't try to train against breed. No breed is good at everything.

Nancy Winters

It is by no means necessary that your husband should be a *facsimile* of yourself.

"H.W.H.," *How to Choose a Husband*, 1856

Like most susceptible little women; I have a surrendering weakness for Professional Men. Most childishly weak for Doctors . . . one so trained in the body's displeasures; must consequently professionally understand: what are the body's exact technical pleasures.

Caitlin Thomas

I must admit to having a covert passion for men in threadbare Shetland jumpers.

Rowan Pelling

How to *Choose* a Mate

Power and ruthlessness in a man have ever appealed to women.

Ilka Chase, *Past Imperfect*, 1943

What a man has to say about his ex says everything about himself. It is a gift, a trailer for a movie you may yet decide you don't want to see.

Barbara Ellen

All my husbands were macho: a bunch of elk with big antlers. Alpha Males. All of them.

Jane Fonda

Look for a sweet person. Forget rich.

Estée Lauder

I'd like to marry a nice domesticated homosexual with a fetish for wiping down formica and different vacuum-cleaner attachments. Preferably one who could give a good shoulder rub and has an American passport. Is that too much to ask?

Jenny Eclair

Not unfrequently it is your ideal which you can make a certain man fill. Often, if you are not blinded, you will see that instead of filling it, he "wobbles" around in the large space you have given him. That ideal can easily be transferred to another man.

Irene Hartt, *How to Get Married, Though a Woman*, 1895

Mutual *Delight*

One of the chief stations on this rail in the journey of life is *Marriage*. Some people reach it too soon; some too late; some never. Those who get there too soon often find they have not made proper provision for the journey, and therefore feel the pinch, and serve them right. Those who get there too late lose much of pleasure and benefit of the journey.

Another of the stations – before you get to *Marriage* – is *Courtship*; and a very pleasant one it is. You will be glad of some refreshment there, and several pretty girls will only be too ready to hand it to you, and let you pay well for it. You should not loiter too long here, or drink too much; for if you become tipsy and jolly and do not know what you are about, you may get into the wrong train, and not find out your mistake till you reach the next station; and this turns out to be *Fornication* or *Adultery*.

Henry Butter, *Marriage for the Million*, 1872

There are several early warning signs that you've found the perfect someone. Your brain will leave on an extended holiday while your mouth adopts a constant smile.

Aubrey Malone

Courting iz like 2 little springs ov soft water that steal out from under a rock at the fut ov a mountain and run down the hill side by side singing and dansing and spatering each uther, eddying and frothing and kaskading, now hiding under bank, now full ov sun and now full ov shadder, till bimeby tha jine and then tha go slow.

Josh Billings (Henry Wheeler Shaw), *Josh Billings' Wit and Humor*, 1874

Every man ought to be in love a few times in his life, and to have a smart attack of the fever.

William Makepeace Thackeray

Mutual *Delight*

All of us are going to probably fall in love with someone and attempt to have a relationship more so than, say, being caught in a ship that goes upside-down or trying to burrow to the center of the earth. It's interesting to play with that because it's the most exciting thing that happens to us.

Julianne Moore

Once you have realized that one person in the world is the best and most perfect, the one you would admire and love for ever, other people are barely even real.

Victoria Coren

At the beginning of a love affair, not even the neurotic is neurotic.

Mignon McLaughlin

Romance is the glamor which turns the dust of everyday life into a golden haze.

Elinor Glyn

One thing that accompanies the passion in its first blush is certainly difficult to explain. It comes (I do not quite see how) that from having a very supreme sense of pleasure in all parts of life – in lying down to sleep, in waking, in motion, in breathing, in continuing to be – the lover begins to regard his happiness as beneficial for the rest of the world and highly meritorious in himself.

Robert Louis Stevenson

The Big Question

Only a salmon or a nincompoop splashes into matrimony blithely.

Helen Gurley Brown

My wonder is that young men ever marry. The difficulty of selection must be appalling.

Jerome K. Jerome, *The Second Thoughts of an Idle Fellow*, 1898

Do not expect the guy to make a hasty commitment. By "hasty" I mean, "within your lifetime."

Dave Barry

They say, "endless emotional demands," we say, "conversation." They say, "This beer tastes great," we wail, "Commitment-phobe" and so on.

Barbara Ellen

Men are like corks. Some will pop the question, others have to be drawn out.

Anthony Cotterell

It is very injudicious, not to say presumptuous, for a gentleman to make a proposal to a young lady on too brief an acquaintance. A lady who would accept a gentleman at first sight can hardly possess the discretion needed to make a good wife.

John H. Young, *Our Deportment, Or the Manners, Conduct and Dress of the Most Refined Society*, 1881

The Big *Question*

It is a happy idea to marry while we are young – a fine thing – a good thing – a pleasant duty indeed – to marry the woman of our choice at a time of life when both are at an age when adjustment is natural and lasting loyalties are implanted in our hearts and minds for all time. We make a sad mistake when we postpone so important a step just for the sake of becoming a rich man first so that our bride-to-be may step into luxurious quarters and never have to lift her dainty hands except to sip from the glass of nectar we have set before her.

Douglas Fairbanks, *Laugh and Live*, 1917

A man must always let a woman do a reasonable share of the courting.

Miss Lena Searlwood, "Platitudes and Pleasures" from *The Inner Sisterhood, A Social Study in High Colors*, 1884

Why should not women propose? Why should they be at a disadvantage in an affair which concerns the happiness of the whole life? They have as much right to a choice as men, and to an opportunity to exercise it.

Charles Dudley Warner, *As We Were Saying*, 1891

Are you, then, to reject all suggestions of a sensible marriage with any man who is not Prince Perfect? I once read a very sensible little poem which described the heroine waiting year after year for Prince Perfect. He came at last, but unfortunately "he sought perfection too," so nothing came of it!

Lucy H. M. Soulsby, *Stray Thoughts for Girls*, 1903

The Big *Question*

A proposal of marriage is all about timing . . . and blood-alcohol levels.

Peter van Dijk

What a clumsy thing is language, what an awkward thing a formal proposal stuttered out by a lover more embarrassed than if he were an amateur actor appearing on the stage for the first time, as Romeo before an international audience of actors and critics!

Henry T. Finck, *Romantic Love and Personal Beauty*, 1887

Ther's monny a daycent sooart of a young chap at thinks he could like to mak up to a young lass at he's met at th' chapel or some other place, but as sooin as he gets at th' side on her, he caant screw his courage up to th' stickin' place, an' he axes her some sooart ov a gaumless question, sich as "ha's your mother."

John Hartley, *Yorkshire Ditties*, late 19th century

The best way is to apply to the lady in person, and receive the answer from her own lips. If courage should fail a man in this, he can resort to writing, by which he can clearly and boldly express his feelings. A spoken declaration should be bold, manly and earnest.

John H. Young

The modern practice is the Proposal Prosaic; in a snack bar; walking down the street; on top of a bus; or coming out of the movies.

Anthony Cotterell

The Big *Question*

Proper proposals are always done on one knee. This indicates to your future wife that you are fully prepared for a life of begging and pleading.

Peter van Dijk

To give her the ring take her somewhere with a starlight atmosphere where you can guarantee being alone together for as long as you want to be. Somewhere where you won't have mother poking her kindly face round the door to be shown the ring.

This is a strictly private moment. If anything is sacred this is. You don't want her kid brother looking for his ping-pong balls under your chair. So go some place you both like; work up a romantic atmosphere, then take the ring out of your pocket, and make a simple, rather formal little speech. Like this:

"Well, darling, here it is. I do hope you like it."

(Put the ring on her finger firmly but not hurriedly. Then take her in your arms masterfully and kiss her tenderly.)

Anthony Cotterell

When a couple gets engaged commonly the girl gets a diamond ring and the guy gets a golf trip away with the boys for a week and a new Harley Davidson. Oh no, that's right, we get nothing.

Simon Hertnon

Marriage requires a person to prepare four types of Rings: Engagement Ring, Wedding Ring, Suffering, Enduring.

Anonymous

The Big *Question*

It is a formidable decision to make when one says: "I bind myself for life; I have chosen; from now on my aim will be, not to search for someone who may please me, but to please the one I have chosen."

André Maurois

At no time in a girl's life has she a greater right to work out her own salvation in fear and trembling than during the period known among girls as "making up her mind." If she is the right kind of a girl, honest and delicate minded, it is nerve-racking to be talked about, and sacrilege to be talked to. . . . Yet these kind friends never think of the delicate, touch-me-not influences at work in the girl's soul, or that the instinct to hide her real interest in the man precludes the possibility of her daring to ask to be let alone.

Lilian Bell

The offer of a man's heart and hand is the greatest compliment he can pay you. . . . A refusal is, to most men, not only a disappointment, but a mortification.

"An American Lady," *The Ladies' Vase: Polite Manual for Young Ladies*, 1849

It is only the contemptible flirt that keeps an honorable man in suspense for the purpose of glorifying herself by his attentions in the eyes of friends. Nor would any but a frivolous or vicious girl boast of the offer she had received and rejected. Such an offer is a privileged communication. The secret of it should be held sacred. No true lady will ever divulge to anyone, unless it may be to her mother, the fact of such an offer. It is the severest breach of honor to do so.

John H. Young

The Big Question

The first love-kiss generally precedes the declaration. But the best etiquette would be to reserve all the kissing for the honeymoon.

Advice to Young Ladies, from the *London Journal*, 1855 and 1862

If it were worth the while, I would advise you not to sit on a man's lap till you are his wife.

Irene Hartt

A lady should not be too demonstrative of her affection during the days of her engagement. There is always the chance of "a slip 'twixt the cup and the lip."

John H. Young

There are strong physiologic reasons against long engagements: they keep the affections and the passions in an excited and unnatural condition, which after a time tends to weaken the nervous system and undermine the health.

Anna M. Galbraith

Deliberate sexual pleasure has no place in courtship. It is forbidden by the Sixth Commandment under pain of mortal sin. . . . Your best guarantee therefore for a successful and chaste union is to keep your dating on a high moral level.

Godfrey Poage

Do not stimulate impure thinking by theatre-going, the reading of salacious books, participation in the round of dance, the presence of nude statuary and suggestive pictures.

Sylvanus Stall

The Big *Day*

The Right Time of the Year to Marry.— When woman marries she enters upon a new life, and a very trying one. Extreme heat and extreme cold are both very taxing to the human economy. Midsummer and midwinter are therefore both objectionable, but especially the former.

Anna M. Galbraith

There is something exquisitely poetical in the idea of a June wedding. It is the very month for the softer emotions and for the wedding journey. In England it is the favorite month for marriages. May is considered unlucky, and in an old almanac of 1678 we find the following notice: "Times prohibiting marriage: Marriage comes in on the 13th day of January and at Septuagesima Sunday; it is out again until Low Sunday, at which time it comes in again and goes not out until Rogation Sunday. Thence it is forbidden until Trinity Sunday, from whence it is unforbidden until Advent Sunday; but then it goes out and comes not in again until the 18th of January next following."

Mrs John M. E. W. Sherwood, *Manners and Social Usages,* 1887

[The bride] should fix the date as far ahead as possible. People, in these days, don't like short notices for anything: and a short notice has a distinct tendency to bring "regrets": the wedding present list slumps accordingly. . . . Diametrically opposed opinions will emerge during preliminary discussions between her and her immediate family. There will be wordy warfare. Your inflexible line though is "The Queen can do no wrong."

Austin Reed Ltd, *How to Get Married*, 1936

The Big *Day*

Most brides are live wires; handle them only with non-conducting gloves, lined with tenderness and understanding.

William Lee Howard, *Facts for the Married*, 1913

It is very pleasant to us to feel that the bride doesn't know what is going to be done to her. Her helpless innocence is her charm.

Mary Borden

Your wedding is about you in the same way that the NBA All-Star game is about the basketball. You are a prop.

Peter van Dijk

Indeed the whole aim of a fashionable marriage, with its long array of carriages, guests, wedding-favours, bridesmaids, dresses, festivities, &c., seems intended very properly to distract the attention of the bride from the bridegroom, who must feel remarkably insignificant.

Democritis Machiavel Brown (James MacGrigor Allan),
*Young-Ladyism; a Handbook on the Education, Accomplishments,
Duties, Dress, and Deportment of the Upper Ten Thousand*, 1859

Mr.— never would have been accepted if his wife had thought only of him, but a veil and orange flower-wreath, which suits a bride so well, cannot be worn excepting on the wedding day, and, in order to marry, a husband is required; so he is taken as an accessory, just in the same way that carriages are hired. Many would prefer being married without a husband, but that is not the custom.

Alphonse Karr

The Big *Day*

The bride to be must be taken out on the town by a gang of women who know how to breach the peace professionally.

Jenny Eclair

Upon your arrival in the city where the wedding is to take place you will be met by the bridegroom, who will take you to the home of the bride where you are to stay. There you are met by the bride's father. "This is my best man," says the groom. "The best man?" replies her father. "Well, may the best man win." At once you reply, "Ha! Ha! Ha!"

Donald Ogden Stewart on the duties of the best man,
Perfect Behavior, 1922

34

The Stag night should be held sufficiently in advance of the wedding to allow for any prison sentences that might have to be served as a result.

Jenny Eclair

It doesn't really matter what you do on the actual night as long as the next morning the intended groom wakes up naked, handcuffed to an orang-utan, in a cage in the hold of a Boeing 747 which has just landed in Jakarta.

Adrian Edmondson, Mark Leigh and Mike Lepine

If you're a man have your hair cut not the day before the wedding, but a week before the wedding; avoid that just-out-of-Dartmoor [prison] touch.

Anthony Cotterell

The Big *Day*

To men of a shyer and more nervous temperament, to be married without chloroform is a very painful operation.

Reverend E. J. Hardy

Weddings are not only unions but also separations from family members. Strange as this may seem, that's why marriage rituals are quite close in many cultures to those of funerals.

Darian Leader

A wedding is just like a funeral except that you get to smell your own flowers.

Grace Hansen

It is not etiquette, at a wedding or wedding reception, to congratulate the bride; it is the bridegroom who receives congratulations; the bride, wishes for her future happiness.

Sarah Annie Frost, *Frost's Laws and By-Laws of American Society*, 1869

Weeks are generally required in preparation for an up-to-date wedding; months are necessary in recovering from such an affair. Indeed, some of the participants, notably the bride and groom, never quite get over the effects of a marriage.

Donald Ogden Stewart

If people keep pushing "tradition" on you, tell them you've decided to adopt the ancient tradition of the Aztecs, who sacrificed the bride's family's first-born son and ate his liver over their wedding altar.

Peter Downey

The Big *Day*

Thousands plight their troth with the most reprehensible levity. With them marriage is a mere matter of course, a thing of merriment – a gala day . . .

"H.W.H."

When you get married have it done right. Don't go frisking out to a suburban justice of the peace to have the knot tied without trouble and without ceremony. Next to your birth and your death it's the most important event of your life. I have noticed that these fly-by-night, "let's-go-out-and-get-married" weddings are responsible for a large proportion of divorce cases in our courts. It's like the come-easy, go-easy money of the gambler. You ought to get the idea of the solemnity and responsibility of marriage pumped into yourself and your sweetheart until you are both saturated with it.

Casper S. Yost

No woman is worthy to be a wife who on the day of her marriage is not lost absolutely and entirely in an atmosphere of love and perfect trust; the supreme sacredness of the relation is the only thing which, at the time, should possess her soul. Is she a bawd that she should bargain?

Elbert Hubbard, *Love, Life & Work, Being a Book of Opinions Reasonably Good-Natured Concerning How to Attain the Highest Happiness for One's Self with the Least Possible Harm to Others*, 1906

When two people are under the influence of the most violent, most insane, most delusive, and most transient of passions, they are required to swear that they will remain in that excited, abnormal, and exhausting condition continuously until death do them part.

George Bernard Shaw, preface to *Getting Married*, 1908

The Big *Day*

"Mommy, where are we? What's going on?" "Sweetheart, we're at a wedding. You see that woman? . . . She's wearing white. White is the color of everything that is happy; she's going to be so happy for the rest of her life." "But Mommy, why is the man wearing black?"

Gene Simmonds

All the fuss, the wedding breakfast, the crowds of guests, the champagne, it is all to celebrate the loss of her virginity. . . . I don't like the mixture of pagan ritual and puritan modesty. I don't like the sly innuendoes, the cheap camouflage, the secretive insistence on the sacrificial drama, and I don't like the way the girl child is got ready for the sacrifice. The heathen are more honest and more dignified.

Mary Borden

No wedding party is complete without the following . . .
1 bridesmaid who talks "Southern."
1 bridesmaid who met Douglas Fairbanks once.
1 usher who doesn't drink anything.
9 ushers who drink anything.

Donald Ogden Stewart

Many a man on the day of his marriage responds to too frequent toasts. Some drink wine at the wedding feast. Now, if there is any time in a man's career when he needs to be clear-headed and unaroused in his animal nature, it is upon his wedding day. The coarse actions, harsh words, frightening impulses, which have often destroyed a wife's hopes, have had their origin in over-stimulation at the wedding supper.

William Lee Howard

The Honey*moon*

Tradition has it that the planning of the honeymoon is the only part of the wedding festivities that is fully the groom's responsibility. That means that, traditionally, honeymoons were the most ill-considered and shabbily planned part of the entire process.

Peter van Dijk

After the turmoil and excitement of the wedding are over and the bride and groom start off on their honeymoon, the first thing that confronts them is the fact that they are alone.

M. Esther Harding, *The Way of All Women: A Psychological Interpretation*, 1933

The first part of our marriage was wonderful. But then on the way back from the ceremony . . .

Henny Youngman

The ordinary kind of honeymoon seems as if it had been expressly contrived to bring to light, and even magnify, any little faults of temper, disposition, and so on, which had lain hid throughout the golden hours of courtship. It is, in short, too great a trial for ordinary human nature. . . . Unless you are very certain both of yourself and of your wife, you would do well to make the honeymoon shorter than the regulation month.

Lucas Lovibond, *The Married Man's Mentor*, 1899

Whatever you do, don't go fishing on the honeymoon. . . . No woman in the world really wants to compete with a fish for interest, because she knows she'll lose.

Anne B. Fisher

The Honey*moon*

"If ever you get married, arrange it so that the honeymoon shall only last a week, and let it be a bustling week into the bargain. Take a Cook's circular tour. Get married on the Saturday morning, cut the breakfast and all that foolishness, and catch the eleven-ten from Charing Cross to Paris. Take her up the Eiffel Tower on Sunday. Lunch at Fontainebleau. Dine at the Maison Dorée, and show her the Moulin Rouge in the evening. Take the night train for Lucerne. Devote Monday and Tuesday to doing Switzerland, and get into Rome by Thursday morning, taking the Italian lakes en route. On Friday cross to Marseilles, and from there push along to Monte Carlo. Let her have a flutter at the tables. Start early Saturday morning for Spain, cross the Pyrenees on mules, and rest at Bordeaux on Sunday. Get back to Paris on Monday. . . . Don't give her time to criticize you until she has got used to you. No man will bear unprotected exposure to a young girl's eyes. The honeymoon is the matrimonial microscope. Wobble it. Confuse it with many objects. Cloud it with other interests. Don't sit still to be examined."

Advice given to Jerome K. Jerome, The Second Thoughts
of an Idle Fellow, 1898

If the kitten should develop into a cat even before the "blythe days of honeymoon" are ended, it is no wonder, considering the way some young couples spend the first month of married life, rushing from one continental city to another. . . . The lady gives way to fatigue, and is seized with a violent headache. For a while the young husband thinks that it is rather nice to support his Kate's head, but when she answers his sympathetic inquiries sharply and petulantly, he in turn becomes less amiable, dazzling, enchanting, and in a word, all that as a *fiancé* he had been.

Reverend E. J. Hardy

The Honey*moon*

Next to hot chicken soup, a tattoo of an anchor on your chest, and penicillin, I consider a honeymoon one of the most overrated events in the world.

Erma Bombeck

After the celebration, newlyweds can finally relax and enjoy marital bliss with San Clemente Palace's Venetian Honeymoon package. The offer includes three nights in a deluxe double room: daily buffet breakfast; bouquet of flowers, basket of fresh fruit and a bottle of Spumante Brut in-room upon arrival; candlelit dinner in the resort's "Ca' dei Frati" restaurant, which features romantic views of the lagoon (accompanied by wines selected by the sommelier); dinner at the famous "Antico Martini" restaurant, accompanied by wines selected by the sommelier (courtesy of the hotel); a gondola promenade; facial, manicure and pedicure for the bride and anti-stress treatment for the groom.

The brochure for the San Clemente Palace Hotel, in Venice, 2005
(the building was once the town's female lunatic asylum)

As a preparation for normal everyday married life, the honeymoon has no value at all, simply because at its best, when it is a tremendous success, it is no more normal than a drinking bout or any other extravagant form of self-indulgence.

Mary Borden

All the world may love a lover, but I am sure that all the world hates a newly married couple that conducts its post-nuptial courtship so that all who see may snigger.

Basil Tozer, *The Irony of Marriage*, 1908

The Honey*moon*

Such exhibitions in the cars or in public places as one often sees, of the bride laying her head on her husband's shoulder, holding hands, or kissing, are at once vulgar and indecent. All public display of an affectionate nature should be sedulously avoided.

Mrs John M. E. W. Sherwood

To Fondle and Dally with ones Wife at Table, before Servants . . . is very indecent, a lessening of the Gravity and Stayedness of the husband, and contrary to the Modesty of the Wife. In this case, if the Man wants Discretion to refrain, the Woman ought to have the Prudence to obstruct it.

Don Francisco Manuel de Mello

41

I wonder to how many newly married couples the idea has occurred that perhaps they would enjoy being married quite as much or more if they didn't go away by themselves with the express purpose of making love to each other all day and all night for a month or so in a solitude of two, but walked straight from church into the normal life they meant to live together, with the wonderful stimulant of their new exciting love to irradiate the pots and pans, the breakfast table and the office desk.

Mary Borden

He wants to thrill her on the honeymoon? Here's a sure way to do it. Let him tell her he doesn't feel married to her. Convince her that she could hold him without the words of a parson or registrar. Then sit back and watch her blossom out.

Anne B. Fisher

Bed *and* Other Blessings

There once used to be many who thought, and probably there still are some, even here in England, who think that a girl should hear nothing of love till the time comes in which she is to be married.

Anthony Trollope, Autobiography of Anthony Trollope, 1883

Whatever stimulates the emotions causes a premature development of the sexual organs; as children's parties, late hours, sensational novels, loose stories, the drama and the ball-room. . . . It is generally believed that early stimulation of the sexual instincts leads to the premature establishment of puberty, as do also spiced foods and alcoholic beverages.

Anna M. Galbraith

Throughout her girlhood the atmosphere grows thicker. She finally faces the most perilous and beautiful of experiences with little more than the ideas which have come to her from the confidences of evil-minded servants, inquisitive and imaginative playmates, or the gossip she overhears in her mother's society. Every other matter of her life, serious and commonplace, has received careful attention, but here she has been obliged to feel her way and, worst of abominations, to feel it with an inner fear that she ought not to know or seek to know.

Ida M. Tarbell, The Business of Being a Woman, 1921

Confronted by the word "clitoris," there's still a few would guess at one of the lesser-known Greek islands.

Riley in Carol Clewlow's Not Married, Not Bothered

Bed *and* Other Blessings

That "perfect innocence" may be very beautiful, but it is a perilous possession, and Eve should have the knowledge of good and evil ere she wanders forth from the paradise of a mother's love. Many an unhappy marriage dates from its very beginning, from the terrible shock to a young girl's sensitive modesty and pride, her helpless bewilderment and fear . . . no mother should let her daughter, blindfold, slip her neck under the marriage yoke.

Annie Besant, An Autobiography, 1893

Going to bed presents a problem of temperamental adjustment so subtle, so tricky, so dangerous, that it calls for the exercise of the most exquisite manners.

Mary Borden

Be it said, then, first, that it is the duty of every bride and groom, before they engage in sexual commerce with each other, to acquaint themselves thoroughly with the anatomy and physiology of the sex organs of human beings, both male and female, and to make the acquirement of such knowledge as dispassionate and matter-of-fact an affair as though they were studying the nature, construction and functions of the stomach, or the digestive processes entire, or the nature and use of any of the other bodily organs.

H. W. Long, Sane Sex Life and Sane Sex Living, Some Things
That All Sane People Ought to Know About Sex Nature
and Sex Functioning; Its Place in the Economy of Life,
Its Proper Training and Righteous Exercise, 1922

Bed *and* Other Blessings

The day of wedding bells, of blooming exotics and friendly congratulations, ends in a night of suffering and sorrow.

> Alice B. Stockham, pioneer of a slow climaxless copulation she called "Karezza," *Karezza, Ethics of Marriage*, 1896

Not seldom is a girl married unaware that married life will bring her into physical relations with her husband fundamentally different from those with her brother. When she discovers the true nature of his body, learns the part she has to play as a wife, she may refuse utterly to agree to her husband's wishes. I know one pair of which the husband, chivalrous and loving, had to wait years before his bride recovered from the shock of the discovery of the meaning of marriage and was able to allow him a natural relation. There have been not a few brides whom the horror of the first night of marriage with a man less considerate has driven to suicide or insanity.

> Marie Stopes, *Married Love*, 1918

It is one of the superstitions of the human mind to have imagined that virginity could be a virtue.

> Voltaire (François-Marie Arouet)

I blame my mother for my poor sex life. All she told me was "the man goes on top and the woman underneath." For three years my husband and I slept in bunk beds.

> Joan Rivers

The chamber of love should be a sanctified spot.

> Martha Careful, *Household Hints to Young Housewives*, 1853

Bed *and* Other Blessings

The following is the situation which the wise men of old have described as being the best fitted for sexual intercourse with women. Choose the largest, and the finest, and the most airy room in the house, purify it thoroughly with whitewash, and decorate its spacious and beautiful walls with pictures and other objects upon which the eye may dwell with delight. Scattered about this apartment place musical instruments, especially the pipe and the lute; with refreshments, as cocoa-nut, betel-leaf and milk, which is so useful for retaining and restoring vigour; bottles of rose water and various essences, and books containing amorous songs . . . whilst both man and woman should contend against any reserve, or false shame, giving themselves up in complete nakedness to unrestrained voluptuousness, upon a high and handsome bedstead, raised on tall legs, furnished with many pillows, and covered in a rich chatra, or canopy; the sheets being besprinkled with flowers and the coverlet scented by burning luscious incense.

Kalyana Malla

A western view of "Mahometan" wedding nights . . .
The ball being ended and the Guests retired to their respective Habitations the Sagois, taking the Bride by the Hand, leadeth her to the Nuptial Chamber and commits her to the custody of her Bridegrooms Eunuchs, until he himself comes. As soon as he is come, after the mutual Civil salutations, he takes away her Veil, and all her Cloths, one after another, but when he comes to unbutton and take down her Linnen-Drawers, there will be a little fumbling and scuffling; for she will be sure to show some little willing Resistance. The next day the Sagois comes to pay his Civilities, & makes them many drolling and frollick Questions.

Sieur de Gaya, Nuptial Rites: or, the Several Marriage Ceremonies
Practised Amongst the Nations of the World, 1685

Bed *and* Other Blessings

Marriage is of its very nature a contract in which you hand over your body to your partner and accept his or her body in return for the performance of those actions whereby new life is generated. In other words both of you will obtain the right to the marital act or sexual intercourse.

Godfrey Poage

Marital intercourse for the sake of procreating is not sinful. When it is for the purpose of satisfying sensuality, but still with one's spouse, because there is marital fidelity it is a venial sin. Adultery or fornication, however, is a mortal sin.

Saint Augustine of Hippo, *The Excellence of Marriage*, 401

Marry for sex? Don't be silly! That's better outside marriage.

Helen Gurley Brown

The majority of women (happily for them) are not very much troubled with sexual feelings of any kind.

Dr William Acton, *Functions and Disorders of the Reproductive Organs*, 1858

One of our principal London physicians lately observed to a lady, that *in nine cases out of ten of sickness, and in five cases out of six of death from consumption among young women, the proximate cause was the want of sexual commerce.*

Richard Carlile, an early advocate of birth control, *Every Woman's Book, or, What Is Love?*, 1826

Bed *and* Other Blessings

With rare exceptions, both of person and of instances, in married life all the sexual aggressiveness is with the male. Wives seldom seek the closer embraces of their husbands. They are generally indifferent; often absolutely averse. . . . The wisdom of the Creator is manifest in the fact that were the wife equally quickened by the same amative tendencies, the male nature would be called into such frequent and continuous exercise that the power of reproduction would be either totally destroyed or so impaired that the race would degenerate into moral, intellectual and physical pigmies.

Sylvanus Stall

We also have a firmer mind, and stronger fancy than women. The filaments of our brain are more stretched and hard, and when we love, it is with greater force and spirit. Women, on the contrary, are of a more inconstant mind, and weaker fancy. The fibres of the brain are soft, and more flexible; and though they sometimes appear to love more ardently, yet they do not feel so much pleasure in caresses as we.

Nicholas Venette, *Conjugal Love; or the Pleasures of the Marriage Bed Considered*, 1703

Women are most lustful in the Summer, but Men in the winter.

Giovanni Sinibaldi

The more a man talks about love to women, the more sex he has.

David Aaronovitch

Bed *and* Other Blessings

There can be but little doubt that much marital indifference upon the part of wives is due to chronic constipation.

Sylvanus Stall

Girls, if you wish to have a clear, healthy, attractive complexion, one that most will envy, there is only one rule to remember –
USE COMMON-SENSE.
Keep the bowels in a regular healthy state.

"Madame Elise"

Note that when a woman has her menstrual period, humours ascend to the eyes. . . . It is harmful to have sexual intercourse with these women, because children who are conceived tend to have epilepsy and leprosy because menstrual matter is extremely venomous.

Pseudo-Albertus Magnus

Passion resides in the woman's right side during . . . the first or light fortnight of the lunar month, from new moon to full, including the fifteenth day. The reverse is the case on the dark fortnight.

Kalyana Malla

It is very commendable for a Woman to Sing to her Husband and Children, and it may be permitted her to Dance, if very young, in her own Apartment; I cannot approve of carrying Castanets in her Pocket, learning wild Catches, and dancing Jiggs; these are all incentives of Lewdness.

Don Francisco Manuel de Mello

Bed *and* Other Blessings

The question is put which of the sexes has more reason to be interested in the work of the flesh in respect to the pleasure obtained from performing it. The answer has always been the female sex. . . . A summary judgment has led practical minds to declare that the woman's pleasure must be greater because the feast is celebrated in her own house.

Giacomo Girolamo Casanova

Sometimes your wife will initiate sex. This will occur either when you walk in the door after completing a triathlon, or in the closing two minutes of a tied grand final.

Peter Downey

The desire of the male is situated in his loins; and the lust of the Woman has its foundation in her navel.

Nicholas Venette

Concerning the Clytoris . . . it is somewhat longer in Summer than in Winter.

Giovanni Sinibaldi

As to the clitoris, this should be simply saluted, at most, in passing, and afterwards ignored as far as possible; for the reason that it is a rudimentary male organ, and an orgasm aroused there evokes a rudimentary male magnetism in the woman, which appears to pervert the act of intercourse, with the result of sensualizing and coarsening the woman.

Ida Craddock, *The Wedding Night*, 1900

Bed *and* Other Blessings

The husband's interest, quite as much as his honour, prescribes that he shall never allow himself a pleasure for which he has not had the wit to awake a longing in his wife.

Honoré de Balzac, *Physiology of Marriage*, 1829

Husbands seem to think that mutual orgasm is an insurance company.

Kathy Lette

Foreplay can consist largely of the words, "Are you awake?" And then it's all over.

Sebastian Horsley

The nipple-nibbling misunderstanding is often exacerbated by the faking fib.

Deborah McKinlay

What is man's part in sex but a perpetual waving of flags and blowing of trumpets and avoidance of the fighting?

Dora Russell, *Hypatia or Women and Knowledge*, 1925

There is a strong argument to be made for men being forced to take an exam in creative discourse before they're allowed to "talk dirty" because most male attempts at verbal arousal leave women wanting to stuff a sock in their mouth.

Suzi Godson

Bed *and* Other Blessings

Men can take any amount of criticism in the bedroom so long as it is unqualified praise.

Sebastian Horsley

I normally award points for technique, artistic interpretation and originality.

Jenny Eclair

It is not advantageous to employ many and various positions. . . . Other positions are human inventions prompted by insolence, dissipation and debauchery.

Artemidoros of Daldis (itinerant Greco-Roman dream analyst
and sex guru), 2nd century BC

Sexual relations between a husband and a wife may *look* and *feel* and *sound* and *smell* filthy and dirty and disgusting and demeaning and immoral and a sin against God, but they're not.

Dan Greenburg and Suzanne O'Malley

It is a mortal sin for a husband and wife to have intercourse with the normal position reversed, because it makes the woman active which, as anyone can see, Nature must abhor.

Thomas Sanchez, *De Sancto Matrimonio*, early 16th century

A good deal of sex is quite amusing. Maybe, especially in marriage, people overestimate the good or bad that serious sex can do.

Hedy Lamarr

Bed *and* Other Blessings

We ought to embrace when our belly is moderately filled, for at such a junction we feel a strange desire to be meddling.

Nicholas Venette

For flavour, instant sex will never supersede the stuff you have to peel and cook.

Quentin Crisp

It should be realized that a man does not woo and win a woman once and for all when he marries her: *he must woo her before every separate act of coitus,* for each act corresponds to a marriage as other creatures know it.

Marie Stopes

Is it gay to say love turns me on sexually?

Sarah Silverman

The enlightened female of the present generation sleeps with an invisible scoreboard under her pillow, so eager is she for high records in the matter of orgasms, hers and her mate's.

Vicki Baum

The left hand should not lie idle on the bed.

Ovid

Love is blind, so you have to feel your way.

Brazilian proverb

Bed *and* **Other** Blessings

Just go into raptures over the things you adore slightly more than the things you abhor.

Sebastian Horsley

Now the one easily understood (and as easily practiced as understood) direction as to what to do by way of preparation for the act of coitus is: *do as lovers do when they are "courting."* And everybody knows what that is! And note this – that *nobody ever hurries when they are courting!* They delay, they protract, they dilly-dally, they "fool around," they pet each other in all sorts of possible and impossible ways. They kiss each other – "long and passionate kisses, they again and again give and receive" – they hug each other, nestle into each other's arms – in a word, they "play together." . . .

   Now, these things, and the likes of these things, in limitless supply, should always precede the act of coitus. It is right there that this part of the first act of this wonderful four-act drama or play should be wrought out, and if they are omitted or disregarded, the play will end in tragedy, with all the leading actors left dead upon the stage!

H. W. Long

The husband must continue his action till he sees the body-hair bristle, and hear the Sitkara – the inarticulate sound produced by drawing in the air between the closed teeth.

Kalyana Malla

Don't spread too much sail and leave her behind nor let her finish the race first. Score your goal at the same time then, satisfied, you can lie, overcome, together.

Ovid

Bed *and* Other Blessings
. . . Aphrodisiacs *and* Love-aids

Those who are expert in sexual intercourse are like good cooks who know how to blend the fine flavours into a tasty broth.

Fangneiji, Records of the Bedchamber, attributed to
Emperor Huang-Ti, Sui Dynasty, 581–618

And put not your trust in Arabian skink, in Roman goose-fat, or Roman goose-tongues, in the arplan of China that "makest a man renew his youth and astonish his household," . . . in pine-nuts, the blood of bats mingled with asses' milk, root of valerian, dried salamander, cyclamen, menstrual fluid of man or beast, tulip bulbs, fat of camel's hump, parsnips, hyssop, gall of children, salted crocodile, the aquamarine stone, pollen of date palm . . . aphrodisiacs all, and impostures.

George Douglas, *Paneros, Some Words on Aphrodisiacs
and the Like*, 1931

Abstain from greasy liquids, as in the course of time they diminish the strength necessary for coition.

*The Perfumed Garden of the Cheikh Nefzaoui, a Manual of
Arabian Erotology*, 16th century

If you make love too much, then you must eat a lot, to keep up your strength.

Plácido Domingo

Regarding chocolate, I judge it to be of a neutral effect [as an aphrodisiac]; a cloying product fit for serving maids; yet possessed of value as an endearment, an incentive working not upon body but upon mind; it generates, in those who relish it, a complacent and yielding disposition.

George Douglas

Bed *and* Other Blessings
. . . Aphrodisiacs *and Love*-aids

How to enlarge the pudenda to a fit proportion, in case it be neither long, nor thick enough. . . . Milk hath many more excellent qualities conducing very much to the enlarging of the privities. Ground wormes steeped in wine, then dried, and lastly pounded with the oyl of Sweet Almonds, is an excellent secret for this purpose: In the same manner may be used Leeches.

How to shorten the Yard being too long . . . let me tell you that are troubled, and would be cured of this redundancy, that you must for a time keep a spare diet . . . for a time bid adieu to wine, and to all things that increase lust, as Pineapples, Almonds, pigeons, and all hot and flatuous things, but rather eat Hens, Lettice, &c. and all cold things.

Of venereal impotency . . . these things must be applied outwardly: a Bulls gall, a Hares gall, the decoction of wilde Cucumbers and the oyle of Nutmegs, with which the genitals are to be anointed, which will wonderfully corroborate and comfort them.

Giovanni Sinibaldi

If envious age relax the nuptial knot;
Thy food be scallions, and thy feasts shallot.

Martial, *Epigrams*, 1st century

A cure for premature ejaculation . . . you must take *galanga*, cinnamon from Mecca, cloves, Indian cachou, nutmeg, Indian cubebs, sparrow-wort, cinnamon, Persian pepper, Indian thistle, cardamoms, pyrether, laurel-seed, and gilly-flowers. All these ingredients must be pounded together carefully, and one drinks of it as much as one can morning and night, in broth, particularly in pigeon broth.

The Perfumed Garden of the Cheikh Nefzaoui,
a Manual of Arabian Erotology

Bed *and* Other Blessings

A good share of your marriage will be made, not in heaven, but in bed.

Anthony Cotterell

It has been remarked that the first requisite to success in life is to be a good animal. Will it seem shockingly unpoetical to suggest that this is also a very important element of success in marriage?

Reverend E. J. Hardy

The more intense the sexual life, the better satisfied we are with existence.

René Guyon, *Sexual Freedom*, 1939

It is only when in bed that a husband is able to discover each night whether his wife's love for him is increasing or decreasing. The bed is his conjugal barometer.

Honoré de Balzac

When things don't work well in the bedroom, they don't work well in the living room, either.

Dr William H. Masters

Bed is often seen as the place to work off feelings of anger, fury and frustration, and sex as an alternative means of communication . . . sex has always seemed to be the icing on the cake to me and it only proves problematic when we confuse it with the whole gateau.

Mariella Frostrup

Bed *and* Other Blessings

In many parts of the world many, even most, men believe that if they don't have regular, daily sex they are going to become ill.

Dr Thomas Stuttaford

Chicken used to be a Sunday treat and now it's just a boring old Monday, Tuesday, Wednesday fill-in. Same with sex. There's just too much of it about to put it at a premium.

Virginia Ironside

Sex is logically impossible after marriage. You have to overcome the paradox of "Not this again" and "Hey, where d'you learn that?"

Emo Philips

So many women these days give very good headache.

Sebastian Horsley

Frigidity may also be a form of revenge against her husband.

Estelle Cole

The average wife . . . will confess that after the first five years of marriage she would infinitely prefer her husband, if he must have one characteristic in excess, that it should not be that of persistent lovemaking but of consistent good manners.

Godfrey Winn

Bed *and* Other Blessings

Excessive venery produces lassitude, weakness, numbness, a feeble gait, headache, convulsions of all the senses, dimness of sight, dullness of hearing, a vacant look, a consumption of the lungs and back, and effeminacy.

Samuel Solomon, purveyor of "the celebrated Cordial Balm of Gilead,"
A Guide to Health: or, Advice to Both Sexes, in Nervous and Consumptive Complaints, Scurvy, Leprosy, and Scrofula; Also, on a Certain Disease and Sexual Debility, 1815

But the brain, and the eyes especially, are very sensible of the great inconveniency that arise from excessive venery. In consequence of it, the brain will melt like ice before the fire, the eyes will grow dim and runny, the head will ache in the morning, and be afflicted with frequent meagrims.

Nicholas Venette

I would warn husbands not to recklessly habituate their wives to a degree of sexual frequency and intensity which they (the husbands) may be quite unable to keep up for any length of time.

Theodoor Hendrik Van de Velde, *Ideal Marriage, Its Physiology and Technique*, 1928

The more women have sexual intercourse, the stronger they become, because they are made hot by the motion that the man makes during coitus. . . . On the other hand, men who have sex frequently are weakened by the act because they become exceedingly dried out.

Pseudo-Albertus Magnus

Bed *and* Other Blessings

If a person has an unbalanced sex life, his sexual desire will increase. Devils and goblins will take advantage of this condition. They assume human shape and have sexual intercourse with such a person.

Fangneiji, Records of the Bedchamber

If amorous desires crowd upon you, sing a soul-stirring hymn, or read the Sermon on the Mount, or pray for help, or think of your mother's pure love.

Lyman B. Sperry, *Confidential Talks with Young Men*, 1896

It might be said that no man of average health, physical power and intellectual acumen can exceed the bounds of once a week without at least being in danger of having entered upon a life of excess both for himself and his wife.

Sylvanus Stall

Coitus should never take place oftener than every seven or ten days. When coitus is succeeded by languor, depression, or malaise, it has been indulged in too frequently.

Anna M. Galbraith

Experience has proven that it is far more satisfactory to have at least an interval of two to four weeks, and many find that even three or four months affords greater impetus.

Alice B. Stockham

In married life sexual indulgence is permissible once a month.

Sexual Relations. What You Ought to Know, *Sunday Times*, Madras, 1936

Bed *and* Other Blessings

If you want sex-appeal raised to the utmost point, there is only one way of doing it and that is by clothes. The Victorian woman was a masterpiece of sex-appeal from head to foot. Everything about her was a guilty secret.

George Bernard Shaw

I would suggest that all ardent young lovers, who are about to embark on this difficult experiment, begin by getting rid of that cumbersome, fearsome, unhealthy and unlovely thing the double bed, with all that it stands for.

Mary Borden

Separate beds prevent the desire for excessive sexual intercourse. Avoid the road that leads to the death of desire!

Estelle Cole

The man should altogether cease to sleep in privacy with his wife. Little reflection is needed to show that the only possible motive for privacy between man and wife is the desire for sexual enjoyment. . . . Whenever they feel a prompting for enjoyment, they should bath in cold water, so that the heat of passion may be cooled down and be refined into the energy of virtuous activity.

Gandhi

If the husband cannot properly control his amorous pro-pensities they had better by all means occupy separate beds and different apartments, with a lock on the communicating door, the key in the wife's possession.

Mrs E. B. Duffey, *What Women Should Know*, 1873

Bed *and* Other Blessings

It is extremely unhealthy. . . . Where two persons occupy the same bed, each must absorb to a great extent the exhalations of the other's body. This fact alone, apart from the danger of the stronger absorbing vital and nervous force to the injury of the weaker, ought to be sufficient to condemn the system as insanitary.

Alexander A. Philip and H. Robertson Murray, *Knowledge a Young Husband Should Have*, c. 1910

The man who sleeps alone is his own master. He can pile as many or as few clothes on the bed as he likes. If he wants to sprawl right across the bed or sleep with his feet on the pillow, he can. Give him a bedfellow and the scene changes. Someone is in the way all the time. He is no longer King of the Clothes.

Anthony Cotterell

Bed is the poor man's opera.

Italian proverb

Is there a man who knows what he looks like and what he does when he is asleep? . . . Most people remind one of the gargoyles of Michelangelo, sticking out their tongues at the passers-by.

Honoré de Balzac

Snorers are like mothers-in-law; very funny until you come into contact with the problem yourself. After that it isn't funny. An American wife who can prove her husband snores can get a divorce any time she likes. In Reno they understand.

Anthony Cotterell

Two *into* One

Saying "my wife" feels really different from saying "my girlfriend."

Peter van Dijk

Marriage is our last, best chance to grow up.

Joseph Barth

Marriage is the operation by which a woman's vanity and a man's egotism are extracted without an anaesthetic.

Helen Rowland, *A Guide to Men*, 1922

After all, matrimony is like a mushroom. The only way to ascertain whether it is the genuine article or poison that you have got is to swallow it – and wait.

Max O'Rell (Paul Blouet), *Her Royal Highness Woman and His Majesty Cupid*, 1901

The experience of wedded life is alarmingly like that of dying – each man and woman must know it for himself and herself, and no other human being can share its trials or its joys.

Marion Harland

A long while ago somebody said, "Man, know thyself!" and I would paraphrase that, and I believe, improve it, by saying, "Man, know thy wife!" It's much more important.

Casper S. Yost

Two *into* One

No matter how deeply a marriage may have been desired, it will always be rather difficult for a man and a woman to find their equilibrium. No matter how deeply in love and how intelligent they may be, they will find themselves, at least during the first days, in the presence of a stranger who is going to be infinitely surprising.

André Maurois

I know that marriage is a legal and religious alliance entered into by a man who can't sleep with the window shut and a woman who can't sleep with the window open.

Ogden Nash, "I Do, I Will, I Have," 1948

Marriage is one long conversation, chequered by disputes.

Robert Louis Stevenson, *Essays of Robert Louis Stevenson*, 1906

Marriage is an attempt to solve problems together which you didn't even have when you were on your own.

Eddie Cantor

It is a mistake, of course, to think of marriage merely as an instrument of retaliation. That is but one of the minor benefits to be enjoyed.

Nina Farewell

Why does a woman work ten years to change a man's habits and then complain that he's not the man she married?

Barbra Streisand

Two *into* One

Someone asked me why women don't gamble as much as men do. . . . In fact, women's total instinct for gambling is satisfied by marriage.

Gloria Steinem

My marrid friends, listen to me: If you treat your wives as though they were perfeck gentlemen – if you show 'em that you have entire confidence in them – believe me, they will be troo to you most always.

Artemus Ward (Charles Farrar Browne),
"O'Bourcy's 'Arrah-Na-Pogue,'" late 19th century

Marriage is primal stuff – two people confronting their own mortality. It is not for the faint of heart. It is not for beginners.

Erica Jong

Every lover makes an object of his beloved when he does not make a partner of her in all his activities.

Fritz Künkel, *Let's Be Normal! The Psychologist Comes to His Senses*, 1936

Between husband and wife there should be no question as to *meum* and *tuum*. All things should be in common between them, without any distinction or means of distinguishing.

Martin Luther, *Table Talk*, 1566

My is a selfish little word; one had better practise saying *our, our, our* while still single, then it would be less difficult.

Anna Longshore-Potts

Two *into* One

We often hear from a wife or a husband remarks like these: "I only half enjoyed it, because he (or she) wasn't there" . . . for a sympathetic couple are to such a degree one that a pleasure which comes to either singly can only be half enjoyed, and even this half-joy is lessened by the consciousness of what the other is losing.

Abby Morton Diaz, *A Domestic Problem, Work and Culture in the Household*, 1895

Now, when two people of any grit and spirit put their fortunes into one, there succeeds to this comparative certainty a huge welter of competing jurisdictions. It no longer matters so much how life appears to one; one must consult another. . . . How, then, in such an atmosphere of compromise, to keep honour bright and abstain from base capitulations?

Robert Louis Stevenson

Perfect unity on essentials means that on the broad question of their common life there is unanimity of view. . . . Perfect freedom in non-essentials means that it is not absolutely necessary for husband and wife to like the same book, the same picture, the same play, place or person.

William George Jordon, *Little Problems of Married Life*, 1910

If your loved one is made of honey, don't lick him all up.

Rumanian proverb

Stand together yet not too near together:
For the pillars of the temple stand apart,
And the oak tree and cypress grow not in each other's shadow.

Kahlil Gibran, *The Prophet*, 1923

House*keeping*

Perhaps one of the happiest moments in your life will be when you step into a house which you can call your own home, and for the first time sit down at your own table. If you wish to perpetuate that joy, see to it that you are attentive, devoted, given to a verbal expression of your affection and an appreciation for every effort made by your wife to render your home attractive, your food palatable and your life enjoyable. . . . And as the months and years go by do not think a repetition of praise would become an offending monotony to her.

Sylvanus Stall

A few light chairs of different sizes and shapes, a small lounge, one or two little tables, the floor polished round the edges and covered in the centre with a square of carpet, or, if the whole room be stained, with Oriental rugs where required; the windows hung with some kind of light drapery – what more do newly married couples require in their drawing room? Oh! We have forgotten the piano, and we suppose it is inevitable, but it can easily be hired.

Reverend E. J. Hardy

I wonder how long it would take to name, just merely to name, all the duties which fall upon the woman who, to use a common phrase, and a true one, carries on the family. Suppose we try to count them, one by one . . . though the idea reminds me of what the children used to say when I was a child, "If you count the stars you'll drop down dead."

Abby Morton Diaz

Without a wife the house doth howl.

Hindustani proverb

House*keeping*

An absurd idea is held by some that intelligence and domestic virtues cannot go together; that an intellectual woman will never be content to stay at home to look after the interests of her household and children. A more unreasonable idea has never been suggested, for as the intellect is strengthened and cultured, it has a greater capacity of affection, of domesticity and of self-sacrifice for others.

John H. Young

Cultivated, intelligent women, who are brought up to do the work of their own families, are labor-saving institutions.

Catharine Beecher and Harriet Beecher Stowe,
The American Woman's Home, 1869

The very best Sewing-Machine a man can have is a Wife. It is one that requires but a kind word to set it in motion, rarely gets out of repair, makes but little noise, is seldom the cause of dust, and, once in motion, will go on uninterruptedly for hours, without the slightest trimming, or the smallest personal supervision being necessary.

Anonymous, *Punch*, 1859

A wife . . . should not be besottedly unselfish – and so pander to the man she loves, and make him a selfish brute who will value her less because she has cheapened herself so much. She should not, however, worry him with domestic troubles and incidents, unless they were not caused by her own ignorance and light-headedness.

W. N. Willis, *Wedded Love or Married Misery?*, 1920

House*keeping*

If he won't ever do chores, you may be picking the wrong ones, or have picked the wrong husband.

Helen Gurley Brown

A man thinks that when the woman is in charge she ought to just get on with it and not bother him. A man figures that a woman who asks for his help is asking him to take charge.

Deborah McKinlay

One day's spring cleaning would break the heart and the back of any man.

William Kaye, *When Married Life Gets Dull*, 1911

It is scientifically proven that no woman shot her husband while he was vacuuming.

Kathy Lette

If once we commence a war against dirt, we can never lay down our arms and say, "now the enemy is conquered." . . . Women – mistresses of households, domestic servants – are the soldiers who are deputed by society to engage in this war against dirt.

Shirley Foster Murphy, *Our Homes and How to Make Them Healthy*, 1883

An hour's sewing soothes a woman's nerves. She sews all her little irritations into the seams, imprisons her fancied wrongs into the double gussets, or slays them in the gores.

Reverend E. J. Hardy

House*keeping*

The true economy of housekeeping is simply the art of gathering up all the fragments, so that nothing be lost. I mean fragments of time, as well as materials.

Lydia M. Child, *The American Frugal Housewife*, 1832

Let not two minutes ever elapse between leaving one employment, and beginning another: be as covetous of every moment as if you had only a month of your life left. . . . Never indulge with the Sofa: believe me it is bad for you.

Harriet Martineau, letter to her sister-in-law, Helen Martineau,
May 12th, 1825

There is but an hour a day between a good housewife and a bad one.

English proverb

Most of us have a touch of the Bohemian in us. The intense dislike of most English and American women for housework is a sign of it. It is a relic of barbarism, a harking back to the Dark Ages, when the caveman flung his woman a piece of raw meat for her dinner. How simple it was in those days! No cooking to do, no table to set, no knives and forks to clean. It is quite easy to revert to savagery.

Mary Borden

A clean, fresh and well-ordered house exercises over its inmates a moral, no less than a physical influence, and has a direct tendency to make the members of the family sober, peaceable, and considerate.

Dr Southwood Smith, *Recreations of a Country Parson*, 1861

House*keeping*

Those whom God has joined in matrimony, ill-cooked joints and worse-cooked potatoes have often put asunder.

Frank Schloesser, *The Cult of the Chafing Dish*, 1904

The quality of daily life is what matters, the taste of the food on the table, the light in the room, the peace and wholeness of the moment.

Germaine Greer

Those who are at one regarding food are at one in life.

Malawian proverb

There is no spectacle on earth more appealing than that of a beautiful woman in the act of cooking dinner for someone she loves.

Thomas Wolfe, *The Web and the Rock*, 1939

Healthy nourishment is an incontestable aphrodisiac.

George Douglas

There are but a few things on which health and happiness depend more than on the manner in which food is cooked. You may make houses enchantingly beautiful, hang them with pictures, have them clean and airy and convenient; but if the stomach is fed with sour bread and burnt meats, it will raise such rebellions that the eyes will see no beauty anywhere.

Catharine Beecher and Harriet Beecher Stowe

House*keeping*

A business man who has been at work hard all day, will enter his house for dinner as crabbed as a hungry bear – crabbed because he is as hungry as a hungry bear. The wife understands the mood, and, while she says little to him, is careful not to have the dinner delayed. In the mean time, the children watch him cautiously, and do not tease him with questions. When the soup is gulped, and he leans back and wipes his mouth, there is an evident relaxation, and his wife ventures to ask for the news. When the roast beef is disposed of, she presumes upon gossip, and possibly upon a jest; and when, at last, the dessert is spread upon the table, all hands are merry, and the face of the husband and father, which entered the house so pinched and savage and sharp, becomes soft and full and beaming as the face of the round summer moon.

Timothy Titcomb, *Lessons in Life*, 1861

A married couple who enjoy the pleasures of the table have, at least once a day, a pleasant opportunity to be together; for even those who do not sleep in the same bed (and there are many such) at least eat at the same table.

Jean-Anthelme Brillat-Savarin, *The Physiology of Taste*, 1825

A year's ill-cooked dinners may make all the difference between a man's ultimately becoming a Prime Minister or a clerk in the War Department.

Reverend E. J. Hardy

If the bread in the oven is a failure you lose a week; if the harvest is a failure you lose a year; if the marriage is a failure then you lose a life.

Estonian proverb

House*keeping*

Love is a furnace but it will not cook the stew.

Spanish proverb

Whenever I get married, I start buying *Gourmet* magazine.

Nora Ephron

Cooking is like love, it should be entered into with abandon or not at all.

Harriet Van Horne

Men become passionately attached to women who know how to cosset them with delicate tidbits.

Honoré de Balzac

A woman who knows how to compose a soup or a salad that is perfectly harmonious in flavour ought to be clever at mixing together the sweet and harsh elements of a man's character, and she will understand how to charm and keep forever her husband's heart and soul.

J. Berjane, French Dishes for English Tables, 1931

Those who can, cook; those who can't, wash up.

Julian Barnes

A good cook is not necessarily a good woman with an even temper. Some allowance should be made for artistic temperament.

X. Marcel Boulestin, Simple French Cooking for English Homes, 1923

House*keeping*

When he reads with his wife opposite and takes it she's there just to pour the coffee and keep the toast from burning, you certainly are taking chances with happiness.

Anne B. Fisher

Men love nothing more than coming home to an ordered house, sleeping children, dinner in the oven and a cocktail waiting on the table, but don't necessarily go the whole hog on the conversation that goes with it: "Such a funny thing happened at the playgroup . . ."

India Knight

Who invented that mischievous falsehood that the way to a man's heart was through his stomach? How many a silly woman, taking it for truth, has let love slip out of the parlour, while she was busy in the kitchen? Of course, if you were foolish enough to marry a pig, I suppose you must be content to devote your life to the preparation of hog's-wash.

Jerome K. Jerome

If you're going to be late getting home, for the sake of her digestion and yours, let her know. Women can think a lot of unpleasant thoughts while they watch the food spoil as the minute hands of the clock slip round.

Anne B. Fisher

There are lots of urban legends about cooking and catfood. Sometimes a woman is tempted.

Deborah McKinlay

Emotional *Caretaking*

Continued courtship after marriage preserves the lover in the husband and the sweetheart in the wife.

William George Jordan

The fault with many young men is that they use up all their kisses before marriage.

William Kaye

This is where husbands and wives run aground. They take too much for granted. If they would but see that they have something to gain, something to save, as well as something to enjoy, it would be better for them; but they proceed on the assumption that their love is an inexhaustible tank. . . . So, for every little annoying habit, or weakness, or fault, they draw on the tank, without being careful to keep the supply open, till they awake one morning to find the pump dry, and, instead of love, at best, nothing but a cold habit of complacence.

Gail Hamilton (Abigail Dodge), "A Complaint of Friends," from
The Wit and Humor of America, 1896

Never, never tune out. That is the most dangerous and divorce-producing activity in any marriage.

Helen Gurley Brown

When a wife is left sleepless through the neglect of the mate who slumbers healthily at her side, it is not surprising if she spends the long hours reviewing their mutual position; and the review cannot yield her much pleasure or satisfaction.

Marie Stopes

Emotional *Caretaking*

If you value the person you're with, you have to be aware of them all the time.

William Shatner

If they can, men will fake attention the way women fake orgasms. . . . The difference is, we can tell.

Ariel Leve

It ought not to be an effort for him to rise to his feet when she enters the room. Each of these slight civilities elevates her in her own and in others' eyes, and tends to give her her rightful place as queen of the home and of his heart. She may be maid-of-all-work in a modest establishment, worn and depressed by over-much drudgery, but in her husband's eyes she is the equal of any lady in the land.

Marion Harland

A man never appears to more advantage, than by proving to the world his affection and preference for his wife.

Margaret Graves Derenzy, *A Whisper to a Newly-Married Pair*, 1825

Even though thy wife be little, bow down to her in speaking.

Talmudic proverb

Hug her occasionally when she's not horizontal.

Kathy Lette

Emotional *Caretaking*

Yes, now and then give your wife a present – a real present, which, without involving undue expense, is good enough to compel a certain sacrifice, and suitable enough to make her cheek flush with delight . . . and a little tender petting does her a great deal of good, and may even be better than presents.

Reverend E. J. Hardy

Make a big to-do about anything he gives you – wear it to bed unless it's a toaster.

Helen Gurley Brown

There is no habit more easily contracted than that of wholesale criticism, and it is a habit that grows with fungus-like rapidity.

Marion Harland

The first frown that she receives from *you* is a dagger to her heart.

William Cobbett

There are men – some of them of Christian professions – who take every tenderness their wives bring them, and every expression of affection, and every service, and every yearning sympathy, and trample them under feet without tasting them, and without a look of gratitude in their eyes. Hard, cold, thin-blooded, white-livered, contemptible curmudgeons – they think their wives weak and foolish, and themselves wise and dignified! I beg my readers to assist me in despising them. I do not feel adequate to the task of doing them justice.

Timothy Titcomb

Emotional *Caretaking*

Husband-nagging is almost as cruel as wife-beating. There are women whose perpetual contentiousness is a moral reproduction of an Oriental torture, that drops water on you every ten seconds.

Reverend E. J. Hardy

The husband of "a superior woman" is usually much to be pitied.

Lucy H. M. Soulsby

It is folly for you to suppose for a moment that an angry speech of yours will turn a man from a course of which you do not approve. It will make him hate you, perhaps, but it will not change him.

Marion Harland

Don't ask him a question in the pop-gun, cold-eyed, vinegar-voice style. That scares him right away. He hates to get into the witness-box, and he thinks you are trying to get him there. Put a question to him very nicely. . . . That won't cost you anything. It will, indeed, pay you.

William Kaye

In order to have sunlight at home, it is not enough negatively to abstain from fault-finding and general peevishness. We should recognize praise as a positive duty.

Reverend E. J. Hardy

It doesn't matter if the flattery you heap on him is close to baloney – heap away! . . . Scout around for the good stuff . . . there's got to be some.

Helen Gurley Brown

Emotional *Caretaking*

To *Wives* I say, be as careful to make a cage for the husband as you were to make the net for the lover. Let home be his happy cage, and yourself the attractive call-bird.

John C. Miller, *Courtship and Marriage*, 1861

It will require much pains, but they are pleasing ones, to make the ever-turning wheel of sublunary bliss keep steady to the summit it has reached, or at least to prevent it rolling down the rugged precipice where jealousy, disgust, and grief, have marked the horrid road. . . . Be it your province, then, to keep your husband's heart from sinking into the incurable disease of tasteless apathy. Do not rely too much upon your personal charms, however great.

Elizabeth Griffith, *Essays Addressed to Young Married Women*, 1782

Wives, be wise and retain your reserve. Do not sound the death-knell of your husband's desires by committing to his eyes all your intimacies! If there is no dressing-room, purchase a large screen.

Estelle Cole

Remember, that any disgusting habit on your part will be more offensive to your husband, on account of the closeness of the union subsisting between you.

The Female Instructor; or, Young Woman's Companion

Not very many men who would like women to love them just as they are would like the women in their lives to stop shaving their armpits.

Deborah McKinlay

Emotional *Caretaking*

It may enchant a man once – perhaps even twice – to watch his goddess screw her hair up into a tight and unbecoming knot and soap her ears. But it is inherently too unlovely a proceeding to retain indefinite enchantment. . . . Allow your husband to come upon you only when there is delight in the meeting.

Marie Stopes

Quite a number of men. . . . Have walked out on their wives because of quite small grease-spots on those wives' blouses.

Mary Borden

The man who wants to keep happily married. . . . Every now and then he should have a careful look at his wife and concentrate in his mind on what she is wearing.

William Kaye

It is yet more rude for any Man to rush in bluntly upon Women, without giving them time to appear with Advantage: they do not love to be surprised.

Adam Petrie, *Rules of Good Deportment*, 1720

See to it that you have a pure breath. You have no right to defile your body, or render your breath impure or offensive in any way, and especially by the use of tobacco and liquor. You have no more right to defile the air which your wife is to breathe than you have to defile the water which she is to drink.

Sylvanus Stall

The world is full of divorced men who stood up for their rights and their whiskery faces.

Anne B. Fisher

Emotional *Caretaking*

Marriage is the only war where you sleep with the enemy.

Mexican proverb

They marry expecting to be happy. For love, they say, is a miracle; and if they marry for love, marriage and love will supply their own deficiencies. Selfish, stupid, infantile and bad-tempered they may be; it won't matter. . . . And so they enter on the most difficult, exacting, unnatural human relationship in the world, expecting to be saved from themselves by it, and they proceed to make each other unhappy because they are after all selfish, stupid, infantile and bad-tempered.

Mary Borden

One advantage of marriage, it seems to me, is that when you fall out of love with him, or he falls out of love with you, it keeps you together until you maybe fall in again.

Judith Viorst

In marriage there are no manners to keep up, and beneath the wildest accusations no real criticism. Each is familiar with that ancient child in the other who may erupt again. . . . We are not ridiculous to ourselves. We are ageless. That is the luxury of the wedding ring.

Edith Bagnold

Lovers' quarrels are the renewal of love.

Terence, *Andria*, 2nd century BC

Emotional *Caretaking*

All married couples should learn the art of battle as they should learn the art of making love. Good battle is objective and honest.

Ann Landers

Temper is the salt, the quality which prevents it from becoming stale. Restlessness, jealousy, quarrels, making friends again, spitefulness, all are the food of love.

Ninon de L'Enclos, letter to the Marquis de Sévigné, 17th century

You can't stay with a person you can't yell at.

Erica Jong

How it satisfies me to fight with a certain finesse, and to find that my partner is on the right wavelength.

Colette (Sidonie Gabrielle Colette)

No man ever got the better of his wife in an argument without regretting it.

William Kaye

What intensity of feeling a woman can throw into the enunciation of a Christian name!

Arnold Haultain, *Hints for Lovers*, 1909

Women use as many inflections in speaking these words: "*My dear*" as the Italians do in saying *Amico*. I have counted twenty-nine which convey merely different degrees of hatred.

Honoré de Balzac

Emotional *Caretaking*

A year or two of marriage will flush out the topics to avoid.

Helen Gurley Brown

No subject makes better tinder for marital fights than your mate's former lovers.

Dan Greenburg and Suzanne O'Malley

It is as well to remember that previous love affairs kept to oneself after marriage are like a pie in the icebox – they never give anyone indigestion.

Anne B. Fisher

Bickering is an insidious way of communicating. It's a slow drip, drip, drip which, if left unchecked, can erode the most solid of relationships.

Pam Spurr

Allowed to run out of control, arguing is to romance what Kryptonite was to Superman.

Barbara Ellen

If ever a new and particularly playful kind of torment is invented, I hope it will be reserved for the man who says to his wife, "I told you so."

William Kaye

He who sulks eats his own belly.

Creole proverb

Emotional *Caretaking*

Many a matrimonial dispute occurs, not so much from unwillingness to give up the contested point, as from a dread of being conquered.

Margaret Graves Derenzy

And the so-called brutal honesty of man is only brutal want of tact. That poor, patient, misused word, "honesty"! How sick it must get of its abuse!

Lilian Bell

It is so easy to break a heart; sometimes a mere word will do it.

Marie Corelli

Minutes make hours – tiffs make quarrels; hours make days – quarrels make hatred; days make years – hatred makes separation and divorce. Don't build up on these lines.

William Kaye

Never witness a tear from your wife with apathy or indifference. Words, looks, actions – all may be artificial; but a *tear* is unequivocal.

Margaret Graves Derenzy

A lukewarm apology is more insulting than the insult. A handsome apology is the handsomest thing in the world – and the manliest and the womanliest.

Lilian Bell

Emotional *Caretaking*

Two or three rules for married folk. First, remember the old saying – that all married people should keep two "*bears*" in the house "*Bear*" and "*Forebear*."

John C. Miller

When we experience a lack in our partner's response to us, we should ask ourselves if it is their emotional parsimony or our own failure to realize that we are demanding too much.

Darian Leader

The best means of defense is a volley of soft answers.

Elizabeth Towne, *How to Use New Thought in Home Life*, 1915

Once in a while let your husband have the last word; it will gratify him and be no particular loss to you.

Reverend E. J. Hardy

The man is convinced that if a misunderstanding, a difference of opinion, or the intrusion of undisciplined ego demands, or selfish attitudes have broken the rapport between himself and his loved one, it will be restored if only he can come to her sexually.

M. Esther Harding

If the wife be angry, no matter how little, she will not kiss the face of her husband; the latter should then forcibly fix his lips upon hers and keep both mouths united till her ill-temper passes.

Kalyana Malla

Emotional *Caretaking*

I would say that the supremest lack of men as lovers is the inability to say, "I am sorry, dear; forgive me." And to keep on saying it until the hurt is entirely gone. You gave her the deep wound. Be manly enough to stay by it until it has healed. . . . A man thinks if a woman begins to smile at him again after a hurt, for which he has not yet apologized, has commenced to grow dull, that the worst is over, and that, if he keeps away from the dangerous subject, he has done his duty. Besides, hasn't he given her a piano to pay for it? But that same man would call another man a brute who insisted upon healing up a finger with the splinter still in it, so that an accidental pressure would always cause pain.

If you do not believe this, what do you suppose the result would be if you should apologize to your wife for something you said last year? If you think she has forgotten, because she never speaks of it, just try it once.

Lilian Bell

When it is all past and the sun shines bright again, talking it over and holding rehearsals and post-mortems is unwise. It should be buried from memory forever as a body is committed to the depths of the ocean in a funeral at sea. Let us forgive and forget; if we hold a hurt feeling and adopt a martyr pose we show we forget that we have forgiven.

William George Jordon

Bitterness is like cancer. It eats upon the host. But anger is like fire. It burns it all clean.

Maya Angelou

An eye for an eye only leads to more blindness.

Margaret Atwood

Inner Circles

The phrases, "my husband's relatives," "my wife's family," are seldom pronounced without an accompanying bitter thought.

Marion Harland

It has been said that Adam and Eve started life under ideal conditions because they had nothing to fear from the advice of relations.

Victor C. Kitchen

Interference on the part of relations, in the case of matrimonial disputes, is extremely injudicious . . . indeed, it displays a deficiency of sense, and is a melancholy sacrifice of self-esteem, in a wife, to communicate to others the failings of her husband, or the subjects of domestic disagreement.

Mrs William Parkes, *Domestic Duties; or, Instructions to Young Married Ladies*, 1825

Most young husbands have been known to mention mother's cooking once to the young wife. On occasions it has been said twice. But there is no record that it has ever been said a third time.

William Kaye

Never, under any circumstances, make fun of her clothes or her taste before outsiders. That's a cruel, below-the-belt punch . . . and will hit her so that there will always be a mark.

Anne B. Fisher

Never join in any jest or laugh against your husband.

Margaret Graves Derenzy

Inner Circles

Girls are often tempted to retell their family affairs to some chosen friend, from a love of confidential mysteries; the pleasure of being a martyr leads not only to the communication of moving details of home life, but frequently to their invention.

Lucy H. M. Soulsby

By all means bury your family resentments but don't bury them alive.

Victor C. Kitchen

If you dig your husband about his black-sheep brother, he has a perfect right to call your sister a light-headed gold-digger.

Anne B. Fisher, *Live with a Man and Love It*, 1937

A mother-in-law made of sugar still tastes bitter.

Catalonian proverb

One evil effect of pasquinade and sneer is to put the prospective daughter-in-law on the defensive, and prepare her mind, unconsciously to herself, to regard her future husband's mother as her natural enemy. Many a girl marries with the preconceived notion that, to preserve her individual rights, and to rule in her own small household, she must carefully guard against the machinations of the much-decried mother-in-law. Nine times out of ten, had not this thought become slowly but securely rooted in past years, the intercourse between the two women might be all peace and harmony.

Marion Harland

For *Richer* for *Poorer*

You say stupid things to the person you're in love with, like "Here's all my money."

Sean Hughes

Don't marry until you have made up your mind not to have heart failure every time a bill comes in. Matrimony is an expensive luxury. If you do not think it worth the price then keep out of the game and give some other fellow a chance.

William Kaye

When once a man has entered the marriage state, he should look on his property as *belonging to his family*, and act and economize accordingly.

Margaret Graves Derenzy

When a man says at the marriage altar, "With all my worldly goods I thee endow" and two months later makes it necessary for her to resort to diplomacy to get seventy cents from him to pay the ice man, his memory needs repairing.

William George Jordon

I suppose that the majority of men do not know that their wives hate to ask them for money.

Lilian Bell

There is only one thing for a man to do who is married to a woman who enjoys spending money, and that is enjoy earning it.

Ogden Nash

For *Richer* *for* *Poorer*

A Woman ought to handle Money with as much caution as she would a Sword, or Fire, or any other thing she ought to be afraid of.

Don Francisco Manuel de Mello

Next to sexual incompatibility, economic maladjustment is the greatest bugbear in married life.

Estelle Cole

Since marriage isn't forever anymore, real commitment comes after the fact: when you burn the prenup.

Erica Jong

This would be a much better world if more married couples were as deeply in love as they are in debt.

Earl Wilson

It is easy to halve the potato where there is love.

Irish proverb

Thrift is the really romantic thing; economy is more romantic than extravagance . . . more poetic. Thrift is poetic because it is creative.

G. K. Chesterton

You can achieve an atmosphere of great luxury by buying two copies of the same evening paper so that you have one each. It costs just 1d, but it makes you feel like a Rockefeller.

Anthony Cotterell

Parenting

When a woman enters into the state of matrimony, she would do well to take two spoonfuls of the Cordial Balm of Gilead each morning and evening, to promote conception.

Samuel Solomon

The whole business of reproduction lacks romance these days. Having babies is no longer about getting it on with someone you love and hoping for the best, but all about timing and work and career trajectories. It has become something to be squeezed in right at the end, before your eggs actually keel over and conk out.

India Knight

Many pregnant women are more than usually passionate during the period of gestation. This is especially the case when the wife is happy in her condition, when she rejoices with exceeding great joy that she is on the way to experience the divine crown of wifehood – maternity! When such a woman desires her husband in love's embrace, it is cruel to deprive her of her longed-for delight.

H. W. Long

For a parent, there are few greater pleasures than observing just how abominably badly everyone else is bringing up their children.

James Delingpole

The pressure of having even one child is enough to turn most partnerships into a Swat team finely tuned to your child's needs and for whom romance is a time-consuming distraction.

Mariella Frostrup

Parenting

A wife, who had first spoiled her husband atrociously and then completely dethroned and isolated him, in order to spoil her children, once said to me, "I wonder why having children should make marriages unhappy?"

Phyllis Bottome

One of the greatest wrongs that any parent can do to any child is to victimize him by an undue amount of affection during his childhood. As a result, he becomes parasitic.

Estelle Cole

It would do no harm, if mothers would sometimes ask themselves, when looking at their boys, what sort of husband am I educating for somebody?

Fanny Fern (Sara Willis Parton), *New York Ledger*, 1863

My feeling is it's important to have two people to play good-cop bad-cop at home, and then swap roles when the offspring least expect it. Keeps them on their toes.

Kate Muir

A mother's job is to be an embarrassment. I do that very well.

Annie Lennox

"Do less" should be every mother's mantra. Do less – and make sure that what is done is properly valued at current market prices.

Yvonne Roberts

Forsaking *All* Others

Marriage is like a besieged fortress: those who are outside want to come in, and those already in want to be out.

Arabian proverb

There should be no secrets between man and wife. A woman should never have a confidant who knows more about her affairs, and the feelings of her innermost heart, than her husband. The moment a husband discovers that there is anybody in the world more in his wife's confidence than himself, from that moment the axe is laid to the root of domestic happiness. And so in the converse.

John C. Miller

If a man does a thing he can't tell his wife about, he is doing wrong. If he can't take his wife into all his works and doings, he is abusing her confidence and his own self-esteem.

William Kaye

The enemies of love are not the attractive work colleague or the sexy fitness trainer, the drinking companions or the mother-in-law. These are just viruses looking for something to infect.

Lesley Garner

In a mild form jealousy is inseparable from real love. It is the heart's guardianship of its treasure.

William George Jordon

I believe the wife should do her best never to suspect her husband of being in mischief.

Charlotte Mary Yonge

Forsaking *All* Others

Men and women who are insecure and untrusting enough to invade their lovers' private correspondence never find good news.

Irma Kurtz

Adultery makes a hero of no one.

Julie Burchill

Next to the sudden revelation of one's betrayal, what is most cruel to a man or woman who has been betrayed is looking back on the past, seeing all those years abruptly foreshortened and finding the memory of them embittered.

Léon Blum, *On Marriage*, 1907

Indeed, there are certain women who are never to be enjoyed, however much a man may be tempted . . . a woman living chastely or virtuously with her husband . . . the wife of our friend . . . the wife of our foe.

Kalyana Malla

It destroys a Man's Body. It ruins his Estate. It sinks his Name and Reputation, and procures him Shame and Disgrace. It often destroys their Posterity. It ruins the Soul, and Hardens the Heart.

Adam Petrie on violating the marriage bed

An adulterer who is prepared to repent should sit in an icy river for the time that elapsed from the moment he first spoke to the woman until he consummated the affair. If it is summer, he should instead sit on an ant hill.

Sefer Hassidim (Ashkenazi Jewish Book), 13th century

Forsaking *All* Others

It is curiosity which makes a man who is inured to vice inconstant. If all women had the same looks and the same mental characteristics, a man would not only never be inconstant, he would never even fall in love.

Giacomo Girolamo Casanova

I have no patience with those people who fall in love with forbidden property and give as their excuse, "I couldn't help it."

Lilian Bell

It's enough to make you marvel at what a strange helpless species men are — which part of the body will be "beyond their control" next. A bit like women saying, "Oh no, my breasts just ran out of the door and pressed themselves against Thierry Henry and I just couldn't stop them."

Barbara Ellen (Thierry Henry is a French football player)

A monogamous guy is like a bear riding a bicycle: he can be trained to do it but he would rather be in the woods, doing what bears do.

Garrison Keillor

There is no hocus pocus that can possibly be devised with rings and veils and vows and benedictions that can fix either a man's or a woman's affections for twenty minutes, much less twenty years.

George Bernard Shaw

Men are inclined to crave variety and novelty. A woman must be aware of this tendency — and sexy and crafty and unpredictable enough to counteract it.

Jay McInerney

Forsaking *All* Others

You'll always have the women who are willing to live within the Judeo-Christian institutions, like marriage, with the official sanctions. Then you have the women who are the pagan outlaws. There's a fantastic sizzle for the man, going between them.

Camille Paglia

The wife bears witness to the embryo who was. Even if she doesn't confront him, he looks into those memory-bank eyes and recalls his faults, failures, fears. The new woman offers a testimonial to what he has become.

Gail Sheehy

It is mostly women who are married to men in the public eye who do Standing By Your Man . . . letting the press and public see that you are a twenty-year-older but otherwise exact replica of another woman . . . who the man has been Lying By.

Deborah McKinlay

That Woman that will entertain mean and low thoughts of her Husband will be easily induced to love another.

Hannah Woolley

No matter how happily a woman may be married, it always pleases her to discover that there is a nice man who wishes that she were not.

H. L. Mencken

A woman who is Having an Affair does a lot of the same things as a man who is Having an Affair, except that she is more likely to say "You obviously didn't care at all" than "It just happened."

Deborah McKinlay

Post*scripts*

It is, indeed, the secret scandal of Christendom, at least in the Protestant regions, that most men are faithful to their wives.

H. L. Mencken

Can one always desire one's wife?
Yes.
It is as absurd to pretend that it is impossible always to love the same woman as to say that a famous artist needs several violins to play a piece of music.

Honoré de Balzac

Monogamy is, most appealingly, an energy-saving device which prevents you wasting time and effort on hunting new prey, deceiving a partner or curing a broken heart or bruised ego.

Cristina Odone

I do think it's possible to be monogamous long term. I think it's because whoever it is becomes your favourite person in the world. It's like fifth gear, when you're driving a car.

Stockard Channing

To marry is to domesticate the Recording Angel. Once you are married, there is nothing left for you, not even suicide, but to be good.

Robert Louis Stevenson